Rafael Gomes Sentone
Ricardo Martins Souza
Francielle Hoflinger

Military Police Activity in Brazil

Rafael Gomes Sentone
Ricardo Martins Souza
Francielle Hoflinger

Military Police Activity in Brazil

Effects of police work after night shift on military police officers in Paraná

ScienciaScripts

Imprint
Any brand names and product names mentioned in this book are subject to trademark, brand or patent protection and are trademarks or registered trademarks of their respective holders. The use of brand names, product names, common names, trade names, product descriptions etc. even without a particular marking in this work is in no way to be construed to mean that such names may be regarded as unrestricted in respect of trademark and brand protection legislation and could thus be used by anyone.

Cover image: www.ingimage.com

This book is a translation from the original published under ISBN 978-3-330-76184-1.

Publisher:
Sciencia Scripts
is a trademark of
Dodo Books Indian Ocean Ltd. and OmniScriptum S.R.L publishing group

120 High Road, East Finchley, London, N2 9ED, United Kingdom
Str. Armeneasca 28/1, office 1, Chisinau MD-2012, Republic of Moldova, Europe
Managing Directors: Ieva Konstantinova, Victoria Ursu
info@omniscriptum.com

Printed at: see last page
ISBN: 978-620-8-37968-1

SUMMARY

CHAPTER 1

INTRODUCTION

Brazil is a country in South America, with 26 states and a federal district, home to the Brazilian capital (Brasilia), with a land area of 8.5 million square kilometres ^{(the} 5th largest in the world) and 207 million inhabitants[1] ^{(the} 5th largest in the world). It has a political system characterised as a Presidential Federative Republic, with its states having political autonomy, the functions of Head of Government and State being exercised by a president elected every 4 years, and it is a Democratic State under the Rule of Law.

The Constitution of the Federative Republic of Brazil of 5 October 1988 is the Brazilian Magna Carta that governs and guarantees the country's sovereignty through its powers and forces. One of them, the Armed Forces, made up of the Navy, Air Force and Army, guarantee the defence of the country, law and order (BRASIL, 1988). The public security of the states is carried out by the federal police, the federal highway police, the federal railway police, the civil police, the state military police and the fire brigade, which work to guarantee the preservation of public order and the safety of people and property.

The state military police carry out ostentatious policing to preserve public order, being in daily contact with the population and directly on the streets, as well as being a reserve auxiliary force of the Armed Forces, subordinate directly to the state governors, i.e. in Brazil each state has its own state military police, working methods, uniforms, equipment, personnel and regulations. State military personnel face a variety of social problems in safeguarding Brazilian life, and carry out their duties 24 hours a day, 7 days a week, 365 days a year, regardless of the weather.

In 2015, Brazil had a military police force of just over 430,000, equivalent

---

[1] Brazilian Institute of Geography and Statistics (IBGE).
http://www.ibge.gov.br/apps/populacao/projecao/.

to 471 inhabitants per state military officer. São Paulo, for example, had around 89,000 military police, Rio de Janeiro 47,000, Paraná 20,000 and Roraima 1,500[2] . Due to its great diversity, Brazil has different terrain, climates, social, political and development conditions in each state, which directly reflect on the behaviour of its population, how it behaves and develops. In fact, we can see that the state police or public security forces around the world are directly confronted with and affected by social problems, and have the power granted to them by the state to stop them, when they conflict with collective and legal rights, and to resolve them.

The fact is that exercising the role of military police officer requires the officer to be prepared to deal with problem situations. This preparation is made up of a multidisciplinary body of knowledge and exercises such as physical training, cognitive training (through laws, norms, guidelines and technical procedures), practical development of police activities, psychological training, technical training (shooting, approach, self-defence, patrols, first aid, etc.). In fact, military police work seems to come up against the very complexity of human coexistence, which is based on life in society.

The military police have accompanied and tried to overcome human development through their policing techniques, new approaches such as community policing instituted in Japan, England and Canada, for example, new ways of carrying out police work in the face of social demands (NETO, 2004) with the aim of better serving society.

During their training and professional life, military police officers (MPs) go through a period of training and probationary periods with simulated work routines in which they carry out police activities in a variety of scales. The most common are 12-hour shifts during the day and night, with a subsequent 24-hour and 48-hour rest period (e.g. 7am to 7pm or 7pm to 7am the following

---

[2] Data from the State Public Security Secretariat and the State Military Police. http://g 1 .globo.com/politica/noticia/2015/07/mesmo-com-alta-de-efetivo-no-   pais-sobe-n-de-habitantes-para-cada-pm.html.

day). The design of duty rosters is prioritised by the demands of police work and not, although this could and perhaps should be the priority, by the quality of the police service in terms of intelligent service (thinking about application according to statistical tables of criminal activity by periods of the day, for example) or the feasibility of an uninterrupted 12-hour working day.

Bearing in mind that the activity in question has specific peculiarities (risk of life, work in the face of social ills, high levels of stress, secular institutions), as well as the fact that the professionals have to carry out these activities wearing heavy equipment, it seems to us that physical and technical training are required to respond to the success of the work, since these tasks can affect the physical, cognitive and shooting proficiency of these police officers, during or after service, due to the prolonged effects of the working day, especially at night (altering the cicardian sleep cycle). The thesis presented in this work concerns the possibility that the extra weight carried by state military personnel during their work may affect their upper and lower limb strength, aerobic and anaerobic capacities, concentration and shooting efficiency.

From a humanist perspective[3] and a democratic one[4] , understanding the effects of this activity can provide better working conditions for these officers and, consequently, for the society they serve, which will receive more effective responses, and it will also be possible to outline better conditions for police training, work and academic programmes, encouraging research to improve this activity. Nevertheless, there is a lack of scientific studies on this specific activity, which was once far removed from society, as Bretãs and Rosemberg (2013) point out when they demonstrate that the history of the police in Brazil is as limited as the scientific studies on them, presenting itself as a fertile cradle for research with openings for social interaction between state police institutions and society.

---

[3] Aiming to promote better working conditions and, consequently, a better response to society.
[4] The aim is to understand how the police work and provide a transparent understanding of their activities.

Faced with dilemmas on all scales of humanity, confrontations between society and public security institutions involving protests, marches, sporting events and mass popular movements.

Within this context, the aim of this work is to contextualise the military police activities carried out in Brazil, by means of bibliographical studies, identifying, through a study in the Military Police of the State of Paraná, the physical, cognitive and shooting proficiency effects caused by the working hours of military police officers.

Paraná Military Police

The Paraná State Military Police began on 10 August 1854 and its history is fused with the history of the state itself. It took an active part in important national events such as the Paraguayan War (1864 - 1870), the Federalist Revolution (1893 - 1895), the Contestado War (1912 - 1916), the 1924 Uprising and the 1932 Revolution. Over this time, the institution has grown in number, with around 22,000 military police and firefighters in 2017, serving all 399 municipalities in the state.

Paraná has a relevant context in Brazil, with an MHDI of 0.749 (UNDP)[5] as the 5th highest, placing it close to the nation's MHDI (0.755 - UNDP/2014[6]), considered to be of high human development. It also has a higher GDP *per capita* than Brazil (31,411 compared to 28,500)[7] , showing that the state has a promising development record.

Figure 1. Source: PMPR Brand Manual. Coat of arms of the Military Police of Paraná.

Paraná is located in the southern region of the country, and its personnel work in ordinary policing through its 27 Battalions, 7 independent Companies, as well as through its specialised Battalions: Special Operations, Environmental, Mounted Cavalry Regiment, Road, Urban Traffic, Border, Guard and Escort. They operate on foot, mounted, motorised (car, motorbike, aircraft, boat) and with the help of dogs to serve the state's 11 million[8]

---

5 United Nations Development Programme in Brazil.
http://www.br.undp.org/content/brazil/pt/home/idh0/rankings/idhm-uf-2010.html.
6   United Nations Development Programme in Brazil. <
http://www.br.undp.org/content/brazil/pt/home/idhO/rankings/idh-global.html>.
7   Paraná Institute for Economic and Social Development.   <
http://www.ipardes.gov.br/pdf/indices/tab_pib_02.pdf>.
8Data from the Brazilian Institute of Geography and Statistics (IBGE).
http://www.ibge.gov.br/estadosat/perfil.php?sigla=pr.

inhabitants.

The Paraná Military Police Code (PARANÁ, 1954) sets out all the nuances for entry and conditions for remaining in the institution. In its article 21, paragraph 5°, one of the conditions for entry and subsequent induction into the military police force is that the person is judged to be physically and mentally fit, since the rule stipulates that this component is essential for the exercise of police activity. Even during their careers, these same components are placed as criteria for professional advancement, and they always have to prove their physical and mental health. Article 102 of the law states that military personnel must be physically, morally and intellectually prepared for the perfect performance of their duties.

At sporting events, for example, large populations gather in small spaces and, in unusual circumstances, there are clashes between the crowds and the security forces, whose job it is to contain them. A football match between the two local teams in the capital of Paraná (Coritiba Futebol Clube and Atlético Paranaense) in 2016 brought together around 40,000 fans for a security force of 700 military police officers[9] , a ratio of 57 fans for every police officer. In an imminent confrontation, the security agents, within their police techniques, will invariably have to use force to hold their equipment (shields, helmets, batons), control the crowd, possibly contain individuals and for this they must be, as the rule provides, physically prepared, since they are already at a disadvantage due to the extra weight they are carrying compared to the fan who is carrying nothing and is still in the excitement of the moment.

According to the Paraná Military Police Procedures for the Use of Force in the Exercise of Duty (PARANÁ, 2015), the police officer uses force in a graded manner according to the techniques and type of threat posed to the

---

[9] Government of the State of Paraná.
http://www.aen.pr.gov.br/modules/noticias/article.php?storyid=88836&tit=Esquema-de-security-for-the-Atletiba-is-already-defined.

security agent. The first stage is the presence of the police officer, who imposes himself in order to curb any illicit behaviour, dispensing with physical contact; followed by verbalisation (stage 2) and contact control (stage 3); in stage 4, physical control is used in order to cease physical resistance. Many of these physical restraints are preceded by pursuits on foot, running, overcoming obstacles such as walls, bridges, vehicles, windows, which in themselves require physical abilities that can be trained beyond normal.[10]

The legislation that governs the PR Military Police makes the importance of physical fitness within the institution clear when we analyse article 170 of the Code, which states that police officers judged to be physically incapable of exercising their profession will be retired. In addition to these everyday factors of military police work, we take into account the gender characteristics of the contingent. Society's conceptions make it common sense to believe that women are weaker than men by nature (Souza and Altmann, 1999) and indeed they are, considering that men have more muscle mass than women, 1-2% more in the upper limbs, but the same in the lower limbs, because men produce 6 to 10 times more testosterone and their nervous system has the capacity for muscles to contract more quickly, which allows them greater power than women (Fahey, 2014, p. 11).

More strength and power[11] give them more ability to overcome obstacles, contain crowds, make arrests, wield a baton and a gun. Faced with these facts, police institutions have seen their female contingent increase every year in their administrative or operational spheres of work, which, regardless of biological components, have to put women who have joined the ranks of the institutions in working conditions and will have to carry out their duties overcoming socio-cultural and biological conceptions, mainly through the

---

[10] A person under the influence of narcotics can be so stimulated that they run faster or use too much force, overpowering a security officer who is in the same psychotropic condition as the active one, but diminished by the clothes of the police uniform and the equipment and weapons.

[11] In physics, power can be expressed as the result of Force (F) multiplied by the Velocity (V) produced. $P = F.v.$

technical nature of physical training and military police techniques.

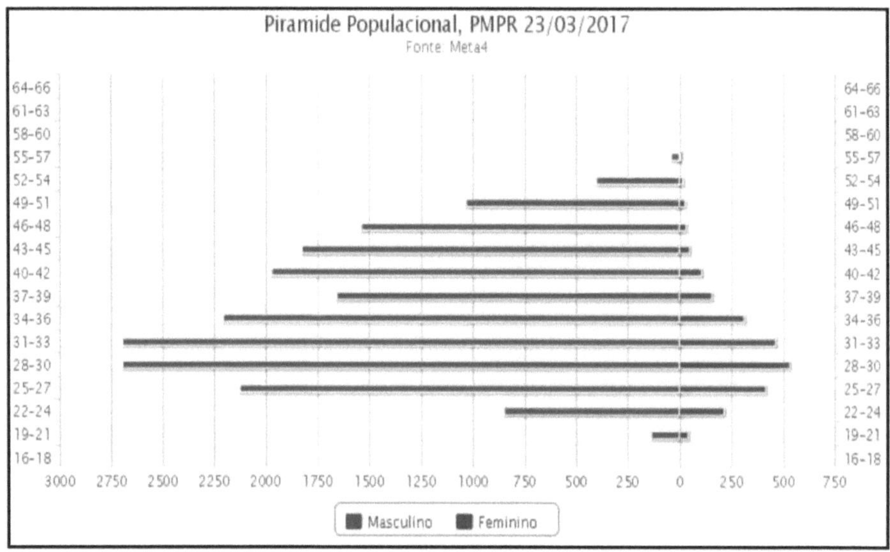

Figure 2: Paraná's military police population by gender and age group. Source: Meta4. Accessed on 23 March 2017.

The reality of the Paraná Military Police (figure 2) shows that its population is higher in the 25 to 36 age bracket, being a young population, with 2,348 women, around 10.5% of the total. This data confirms the importance that the institution must place on physical training for the performance of police duties, allowing no room for inefficiency, possible deficiencies are not pointed out but are relevant in the constructive process of overcoming them.

To give us an idea of the extent and volume of police assistance to the population of Paraná in 2016, 1,307,365 incidents were recorded in the state, around 3,581 per day. In terms of nature, there were 246,279 occurrences of crimes against the person (18.8 per cent), 60,575 adults arrested and 12,725 minors[12] under 18 taken to the police station for referral, all of which could lead to bodily conflicts,

---

[12] Data from the BI - Business Intelligence system. Source:. B.I - BOU.qvw/B.I - DetainedSESP.qvw.

whether it's simply driving from one place to another or fighting and chasing.

Still on the subject of the results achieved by the PR Military Police in their activities with physical performance consequences, according to data from the institution's Internal Affairs Department, in 2016 there were 710 armed confrontations, 637 of which the officer was in a standing position, 37 inside the police vehicle, 15 kneeling, 13 sitting, 7 in other unorthodox positions and 1 lying down, 16.3% of which occurred at a distance of up to 3m, 21.5% between 3 - 5m and 25.3% 5 - 7m[13] . Souza, Momesso and Romanholo (2011) identified through a real shooting simulation with military police officers that heart rate and blood pressure are altered at the moment of armed confrontation and directly interfere with shooting performance, that the stress triggered in these life-threatening circumstances is capable of interfering in the actions of police officers leading to the risk of death because they are unable to control some physiological functions. Storani (2000) and Mello and Nummer (2014) state that military police officers carry out a stressful activity that requires physical and psychological preparation.

The reality of the data reveals the potential of military police activity in Paraná due to the high rates of occurrences, confrontations and detainees. This is in line with the studies presented on the stressful demands of this activity, which requires officers to be physically and psychologically prepared, a reality that can be extended to the Brazilian context and to other public security institutions around the world. The PMPR, like other military police, trains its officers in Military Academies based on hierarchy and discipline, through specific training for the exercise of the profession.

Guatupê Military Police Academy (APMG)

The APMG Higher School of Public Security is part of the State University of Paraná (UNESPAR) (PARANÁ, 2013). has a teaching system divided into three areas: basic, professional and complementary education, with the following courses: Internship, Training Course (CF), Special Officers'

---

[13] Source:. General Internal Affairs of the PMPR. Report on armed confrontations - 2016.

Qualification Course (CHQEOPM), Health Officers' Adaptation Course (EAOQS), Specialisation Course (CE), Improvement Course (CA) and Higher Police Course (CSP) (PARANÁ/PMPR, 1999; PMPR/DE, 2008).

Figure 3 - Coat of arms of the Guatupê Military Police Academy (APMG).

For each course, there are specific criteria for enrolment, as well as duration, qualifications, workload and professional orientation, according to legislation (PARANÁ/PMPR, 2009). Located in the municipality of São José dos Pinhais (SJP), in the metropolitan region of Curitiba, the APMG trains and specialises military police officers and firefighters every year. In addition to the centre in the municipality of São José dos Pinhais, it also has another in the of Maringá, with courses in progress. It has the largest area of the Military Police Academies in Brazil and is also considered one of the best.

The military police training course lasts one year for soldiers and three years for officers, both on a full-time basis. In addition to these, other training courses are held throughout the career, such as corporal and sergeant training courses, training courses for officers, sergeants, physical education instructors, shooting, special operations, negotiators, search and rescue, mounted policing, judicial police, teaching techniques, firefighting, among others.

As soon as they enter the academy, the new recruits experience the harsh reality of military life that they will have throughout their 35-year career when they wear the military police uniform. The military police's own teaching system puts its students through a full course of study with up to 18 lessons a day, 6 in each term, 5 times a week, with the students also having to sleep at the Academy. In addition to the curricular subjects, they undergo instruction and technical visits to state bodies such as Civil Defence, the Governor's Office, hospitals, units of the Armed Forces and the Public Security Secretariat, always aiming to improve their professional skills.

While one-shift undergraduates take between 5 and 12 subjects a year and two-shift undergraduates take between 10 and 20 subjects a year, the Guatupê Military Police Academy's officer training courses, for example, take more than 30 subjects a year, a regime of intense dedication to teaching. In addition to their academic duties, the students take part in sports training activities with a view to participating representatively in competitions, coordinate and supervise the facilities of the academic space as a form of management exercise, and also work on the security of the academic premises since the Academy is a Military Police Unit that also has a police contingent for use in state police activities.

In the normal routine of a military police student, their day starts as early as 6am with activities and lasts until 10pm when they are not on hand to secure the premises, what we call guarding the barracks, or carrying out command and supervisory duties.

This intense and long-lasting routine throughout the training period is accompanied by a process of immersion of future military police officers in their career, which ranges from small activities, services and internships to wearing the police uniform and the gradual increase in what will be their daily lives in the future. The latter, perhaps one of the desires of the newly-included student, is burdened with a weight of responsibility, since representing an institution and this in turn a state, is even greater when we add its physical weight.

Unlike the reality of other careers, the state military not only has its own standardised clothing, coated in symbolism and culture, but also police equipment for protection, action and assistance in carrying out police work. With this reality, students are trained on a daily basis to acclimatise and prepare their bodies in the search for adequate support for the equipment, which is foreign to the social world.

The Guatupê Military Police Academy is a teaching centre of excellence and disseminator of military police doctrine, which has a multidisciplinary and disciplinary character, with physical training being one of the important components for the student in training.

Internship system

During their training, military police officers have to fulfil compulsory internships, just like in other higher education courses such as medical residency or teaching, through operational and administrative activities carried out within the scope of the PMPR. The internships are carried out in the Police Units in the state of Paraná, and the students, as stipulated by the Teaching System through their own sector, under the coordination of the course coordinator, must regulate where they must go. There are various work schedules in the police units[14] where the students can experience the military police on a daily basis, putting into practice what they have learnt at school.

This initial experience is important for police training, giving them a small taste of what will be routine in their future professional development. It helps them adapt to the techniques they learn, which they will put into practice, as well as to the use of equipment, which is very different from that used in other professions, such as different types of weapons, shields, batons, vehicles, etc.

---

[14] Each Military Police Unit regulates working hours according to its needs and the availability of human and material resources. It can be 12 hours on duty for 24 hours off, followed by 12 hours on duty for 48 hours off, or 12 hours on duty for 24 hours off followed by 12 hours on duty for 72 hours off with the possibility of an extra work schedule or instruction on the third day of rest; or 24 hours on duty for 48 hours or 72 hours off following the same criterion of an extra schedule for 72 hours.

The students in training are accompanied by other police officers who have already graduated and are assessed by the policing coordinators of the areas in which they work.

As part of their academic routine, students often have to return to the academy after completing their internship to continue their studies. The internships, which normally take place in 12-hour shifts, demonstrate in practice the struggles of the police service due to the amount of activity involved in the uninterrupted movement of police vehicles along urban, road, rural and waterway routes, whether in ordinary policing, the arrest of criminals and offenders, the expectation of action, guidance to the population and various other activities carried out by the military police.

Unlike normal working hours of between 6 and 8 hours a day plus meal times, 12-hour shifts are a routine part of a policeman's career, requiring adaptability and effort beyond the normal, because military policing in itself requires attention due to the responsibility for other people's lives. All this tension is dissipated in the individual physically and psychologically, and it is common to hear reports of tiredness at the end of policing, be it regular or through an internship.

We are not criticising this process, but merely describing an activity that requires the physical body to have the skills inherent in the functions it performs, and for this it needs adequate preparation.

Uniforms and equipment

In the PMPR there are different uniforms according to the Police Unit, which in turn carry out different types of work[15] , however, there is a uniform in the corporation called organic which follows as a rule for police activity, used by students and military police officers who are in contact with the population

---

[15] The Special Operations Battalion, for example, requires a type of uniform that differentiates it from the others because of the activity it carries out, just as in environmental policing officers wear green camouflage uniforms so that when patrolling in the woods they can camouflage themselves and succeed in catching offenders.

in ostentatious policing.

Figure 4. Source: PMPR collection. Photographer Sdr QPM 1-0 Afonso.
cccccccccc

This uniform is made up of the following items: black socks, tassels, trousers, T-shirt, shirt, jacket, belt and beret; in addition, in order to carry out police work it is necessary to wear equipment consisting of: a garrison belt equipped with a magazine holder, handcuff holder, holster, gun, magazines, ammunition, handcuff, whistle, ballistic vest and a cover for the ballistic vest.

The parts described are basic components, and equipment such as a torch, plastic handcuffs, sprays (pepper spray, tear spray, etc.), weapons of other calibres, pocket knives, tactical pliers, batteries, personal protective equipment (goggles), batons, shin guards, shields, etc. can be added, according to the needs of each police officer and the type of service and/or operation that will be carried out.

Military police equipment is a police officer's working tool and is essential for carrying out his duties. Over the years, equipment has evolved in terms of efficiency, weight, size and usefulness. Weapons have become lighter and have a larger capacity, handcuffs have become lighter and more resistant, ballistic waistcoats ensure protection from ever larger calibres and torches are smaller and more powerful. In addition to their own characteristics, these modernisations are in line with the particular needs of police work, which requires the continued use of these materials, which need to be increasingly resistant. The basic armament used by every military police officer in Paraná is the Taurus model 24/7 or PT 840 pistol, which weighs approximately 1kg, with a magazine and 15 rounds of ammunition.

Activities such as those carried out by the Special Operations Battalion, for example, also add heavier ballistic covers, helmets, shields, batons and grenades. Military police activity is quite practical from the point of view of its execution, which requires officers to be constantly on the move, even at low intensities, but they must also always be ready to make efforts that will always be accompanied by the extra burden of uniforms and equipment.

Operational Service

The operational service carried out by the students in the internships and by the military police officers who have already graduated, in accordance with the work schedule mentioned, normally takes place from 7am to 7pm (daytime) and from 7pm to 7am (night time), normally in pairs and in special cases with up to four officers in the same vehicle. When on duty, the military police carry out their activities in police vehicles, attending to incidents, making approaches, carrying out community activities in shops, schools, institutions, sporting events and repossessions, always in uniform and equipped around the clock.

Operational activity takes the form of rural, urban, water, air, road and environmental policing, among others, in different types of terrain and climate (Fraga, 2006), reaching every corner of the state. Even though they have a work schedule, military police officers do not end their duties by the time of day, but by the end of their activity, often ending their shift after statements have been made at police stations, criminals have been arrested, prisoners have been escorted or investigations have been carried out, which can last much longer than 12 noon.

It can be seen through media channels that police officers are constantly faced with confrontational and risky situations when they are involved in popular demonstrations, whether on the streets or in offices, repossessions, armed confrontations, prison takeovers, hostage situations, high-risk patrols with vehicles, often in low light and under climatic conditions that increase the risk already posed. In order to perform efficiently, these officers need to be physically prepared, among many other aspects.

In a study by Osborn (1976), the author sought to identify the physical components of police work based on Denning's methodology (1984). After observing police officers at work, the author was able to identify the skills required for the job, frequency, specific actions and their characteristics. At the end of the observations and interviews with several police officers, 12 activities were identified that are most developed for the performance of police work: running, jumping, crawling, swinging, climbing, lifting, carrying, pushing, pulling, fighting and dragging. Similar results were found in studies carried out by Ferenholtz and Rhodes (1986), Henderson (1995), Wilson and Bracci (1982) and Gruber (1983), demonstrating that police work carried out in various institutions around the world initially involved the same tasks.

After identifying these tasks, they had to be broken down in terms of the physical abilities that were important for their performance, and aerobic capacity, anaerobic capacity, flexibility, strength, muscular endurance and power of the upper and lower limbs and abdominal girdle were scored (Bonneau and Brown, 1995; Collingwood, Hoffman and Smith, 2004; Hoffman and Collingwood, 2005).

Based on the anamnesis of military police activity, it was possible to understand that breaking through walls, running after fugitives, holding them, stopping them, engaging in hand-to-hand combat, supporting equipment and carrying out so many other exercises during police activity made it possible to realise the importance of police training in the face of so many demands.

Given that the police service provides a high level of stress, muscular and psychological fatigue (Santana, 2012; Costa, Júnior, Oliveira e Euláía,

2007; Gonçalves, 2011) to police officers, added to the fact that they carry heavy equipment for long shifts, generating muscle tension and permanent fatigue, as well as identified cases of Burnout Syndrome in police officers (Guimarães et al, 2014; Oliveira and Bardagi, 2009; Derenusson and Jablonski, 2010) and anxiety, aggressive behaviour, chronic pain and alcoholism (Minayo, Assis and Oliveira, 2011). Knowledge of the load of equipment carried by police officers can give us an overview of the impact on physical performance, and can help to outline the work in question with a view to providing better working conditions, preventing possible future injuries, thinking about better equipment and strategies for the application of police personnel in terms of working time.

Under normal conditions, two individuals could have the same running abilities and strength for different functions, but when one of these individuals is placed at an apparent disadvantage, some strategies need to be implemented to overcome these demands. A police officer under the psychological burden of imminent danger, working hours that disrupt the circadian sleep cycle, deconstructing a childhood, adolescence and early adulthood experience of the concept of "sleeping at night", using their body as a work tool and with the aid of equipment confronting another individual who happens to be in the same situation. Conditions like this are commonplace in the police world and it would be difficult to dispel the common wisdom that police officers need to be prepared for confrontation, which is indeed true.

Some aspects such as adaptation to the activity, the frequency and intensity of occurrences, as well as one's own preparation to carry out police duties, can interfere positively or negatively in the outcome of this work. Some of these strategies orbit around what the individual has control over - such as training, prior rest, adequate nutrition - and are partially out of control - such as the body's biological functioning. In fact, we can say that police work happens at unusual times, under specific conditions and with a high level of aptitude for its resolution.

Physical effects of overload

The reality of military police work is widely publicised by the media in events of global proportions such as the attacks in Paris[16] , the attack on the nightclub in Orlando/USA[17] , the truck driver who ran over and killed people in Berlin[18] and the large demonstrations that took place in the state of Paraná involving teachers and demonstrators, leading to clashes with military police[19].

Figure 5: Demonstration in Paraná/Brazil in April 2015 involving teachers and protesters. Source: Edilson Fogaça Blog. <http://edilsonfogaca.blogspot.com.br/search?q=manif station+of+teachers%3B+confrontation>. Accessed on 17/03/2017.

These are some of the events   involving police officers and society, which required those officers to be physically fit enough to bear the weight of the equipment, handle it and operate it for the hours that followed. Although it may seem simple, the extra weight over time can lead to some significant

---

[16]   Source: NYT. < https://www.nytimes.com/news-event/attacks-in-paris>.
[17]   Source: G1. < http://g1.globo.com/mundo/noticia/2016/06/policia-diz-que-ataque-em-
nightclub-us-left-50-dead.html>.
[18]   Source: CNN. < http://edition.cnn.com/2016/12/23/europe/berlin-christmas-market-
attack-suspect-ki I led-m i lan/>.
[19]   Source: G1. < http://g1.globo.com/pr/parana/noticia/2015/04/professores-entram-
in-confrontation-with-pm-during-vote-at-alep.html>.

losses.

Some studies have indicated that overload during the execution of protocols measuring physical abilities such as movement and shooting, obstacle avoidance, combat running, vertical jumping, lifting and reaching caused a 1.5% loss of performance for every 1kg of extra weight carried, resulting in slower speed movements, longer time to move between two points and less ability to generate force from a standing position (Peoples et al, 2010) and in the order of 1% loss in performance for every 1kg (Holewijn and Lotens, 1992). Ricciardi, deuster and Talbot (2008) assessed military personnel in two conditions: with and without equipment (10kg). The test was a 30-minute treadmill walk and push-ups. The results showed that men performed 61 per cent fewer push-ups and women 63 per cent fewer, and lower limb strength was 16 per cent lower in both when performed with the equipment. At the moderate intensity of treadmill walking 41% of the subjects were unable to complete the test with the equipment.

Similar studies by Leopold and Derrick (1962, 1963), Derrick, Henn and Malone (1963), Lotens (1981) and Haisman and Crotty (2007) found that the correlation between yield loss and extra weight carried can be as high as 2.4 to 3.5 per cent for each kilogram.

Also, according to the same studies, this loss of performance represented slower movement speeds, longer duration to move between points of cover, reduced ability to generate energy from a standing position, earlier onset of physical fatigue during repetitive movements and reduced ability to negotiate obstacles quickly. In the protocols applied by the aforementioned authors, the officers carried out the tests in uniform and equipped. Similar results were found in military firefighters who carry equipment weighing between 22 and 27kg during their tasks, which negatively influences their cardiorespiratory capacity (Carli and Oliveira, 2012).

What is clear is that public security agents work with heavy equipment, clothing and weapons and that for this reason they perform less well in specific physical tasks. In practice, we could have an officer who is chasing a thug on foot, who would be at a disadvantage when crossing an obstacle such as a wall or gate, or who would have to carry a co-worker who has been injured, because the extra weight alone reduces their physical capabilities.

In addition to losses in physical performance, military police officers also have a high cardiovascular risk among men, longer service time and are physically inactive (Jesus, Mota, de Jesus, 2014) and low motor fitness in the variables flexibility, agility, speed, lower limb power and cardiorespiratory endurance (Berria, Daronco and Bevilacqua, 2011). However, it was not possible to find studies that could demonstrate whether police officers show any acute or chronic effect on physical, cognitive or shooting performance after working hours, at any time scale and period (night or morning). The tests carried out studied officers performing tasks with the equipment, but did not show whether there were any effects of police work after the working day.

CHAPTER 2

Physical, cognitive and shooting proficiency effects

SENTONE, Rafael Gomes

SOUZA, Ricardo Martins

The work activities of public security agents have been the subject of research and study, from the way they operate to their impact on society, action strategies, quality of life, technologies, governance and many other issues. In the profile outlined in this book, which focuses on the biological parameters of safety and quality at work.

Some gaps in scientific studies regarding the effects of night work carried out by military police officers, potentiated by the extra weight they carry with equipment and weapons, may reveal some aspects to be improved in military police activity and sometimes clarify the effects during and after the work period. The aim of this study was to assess military police officers from the state of Paraná/Brazil after working a 12-hour shift at night (7pm to 7am) in terms of lower limb muscle strength, cardiorespiratory fitness, agility, concentration and shooting performance, compared to a previous rest period, by carrying out the same tests in an attempt to identify some of the effects produced by these components.

Eighteen individuals (14 men and 4 women), military police officers (30.8 ± 7.7 years old, 79.4 ± 16.8 kg, 8.2 ± 7.2 years of experience), underwent the *"shuttle run"* agility test (LEGER and LAMBERT, 1982), assessment of VO_2 max in the Astrand bench protocol (ESTRELA, 2006), muscle power in the vertical jump (SALLES, 2010), as well as the cognitive test "neuropsychological stroop" (Castro, Cunha and Martins 2009) and shooting test (PMPR, 2014; SPAULDING, 2013). The Questionnaire of Habitual Physical Activity - QAFH (SARDINHA, 2009) was used to control for differences in the volume of daily activities . All the tests were carried out at two different times: immediately after a 12-hour night shift and after a 24-hour break. All the individuals were previously informed about the nature of the assessment and signed an Informed Consent Form to take part in this study. Initially, anthropometric characteristics were assessed in light clothing and without footwear, and in full uniform (trousers, T-shirt, collar, beret, trouser belt, garrison belt, pistol holster, pistol, three pistol magazines, 45 rounds of ammunition, magazine holder, handcuff holder, handcuff, ballistic mesh, ballistic cover).

For the assessment procedures, everyone had to turn up at the Guatupê Military Police Academy at 8am on two non-consecutive days, after a 12-hour period under two different conditions: a) work shift and b) rest break. The order of the tests was: 1) neuropsychological stroop, 2) shuttle-run, 3) Astrand bench test, 4) vertical jump and 5) shooting test. The order of the tests was defined in such a way as to minimise the effects of one test on the other. With the exception of the shooting test, which had to be carried out in police uniform and equipment for safety reasons, for the other protocols the military police officers were dressed in shorts, t-shirts and trainers.The Kolmogorov-Smirnof test was applied to confirm the normality of the data. Assuming a normal distribution, a *Student's t-test* for parametric variables was applied to check for changes between conditions. The statistical tests had a significance level of $p < 0.05$ and were applied using Statística software version 7.0.

Sargent Jump Test or Vertical Jump Test

Its purpose is to measure the explosive strength of the lower limbs. The previously warmed-up test subject must stand next to a wall with measurements from the ground to the ceiling, raise their arm and stand still, and note how much they scored. After this procedure, they must jump as high as they can, raising their arm as high as they can. The difference in distance between the first height and after the jump will be taken.

Figure 6 - Sargent Jump Test. Illustrative figure

Bank of Astrand

The aim of this test is to measure the aerobic capacity (submaximal) of the test subject through the V02max, with the result expressed in -1 ml(kg.min) . Using a 41 cm high bench for men and women, it is suitable for both sexes of university age. The execution procedures were as follows: (a) duration of the test 3 min; (b) stride frequency of 22 and 24 steps per minute for men and women respectively; (c) use of a metronome for stride frequency; (d) at the end of the test, the participant remained still and standing to have their heart rate assessed using a heart rate monitor (FS1, Polar); (e) once the data has been collected, it will be entered into the following formula:

MEN: V02max= 111.33 - 0.42 X HR (end of test)

WOMEN: VO2max= 65.81 - 0.1847 X HR (end of test)

Shooting test - El President

The shooting test took place at the APMG Shooting Range and the *"El Presidente"* protocol was carried out, consisting of a track containing three cardboard targets, one next to the other with a distance of 1 m between them.

The targets have three circular regions from the centre to the end. The shooter must stand at a distance of 5m from the targets with the gun in the holster, safety lock closed and a magazine. There will be 18 rounds of ammunition, 6 for each magazine. At the command of a shooting instructor, the shooter must draw his weapon and fire two shots at each target from right to left or vice versa; after the first 6 shots, the shooter must remove the empty magazine from the weapon, feed in the other loaded magazine and fire another 6 shots (combat reload), two at each target, in the opposite direction to the previous one.

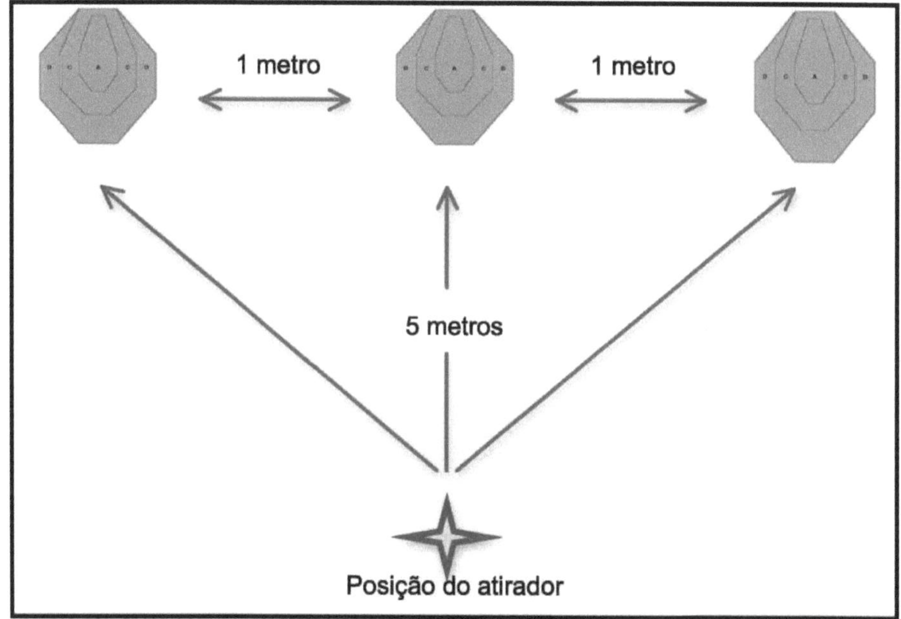

Figure 7. Schematic of the El President shooting range. Created by the author.

When the last shot is taken, the stopwatch will be stopped. The score for each shot is 10 points for shots taken in the centre of the target (A), 8 in the subsequent region (C) and 2 points at the last outer edge of the target (D). The maximum possible score is 120 points and only one attempt is available unless there is an independent failure on the part of the shooter.

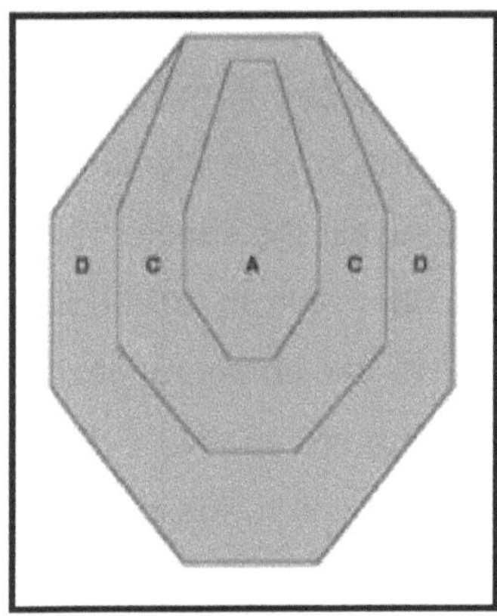

Figure 8. Model of the target used on the course of fire for the Classic IPSC Shooting Test.

Neuropsychological Stroop

The purpose of this test is to measure concentration and executive control or to screen for cognitive dysfunction, used mainly by neuropsychologists. The models used in this research are provided in the appendix of this book.

Shuttle run

The "running back and forth" test assesses neuro-motor agility and speed. At a marked distance measuring 9.14 metres between two points in a straight line, the test taker must run from one point to the other, each time bringing one of the two clubs to the other side. Bringing both clubs to the opposite side will stop the chronometer.

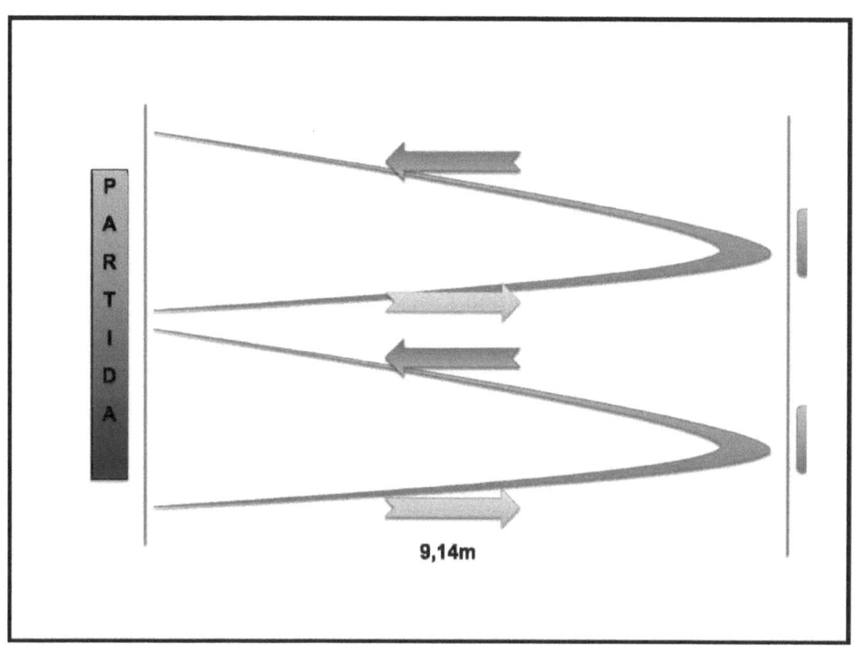

Figure 9. Diagram, layout and distances for the *shuttle run* test. Created by the author.

Discussions

All the individuals performed the proposed tests without any difficulties other than those expected in this type of assessment. No interruptions were necessary at any point during the assessments. With the exception of the shooting test, which was carried out on an open track, all the other tests took place indoors under the same conditions for all participants. The results are summarised in table 1.

Table 1 Results of the physical, cognitive and shooting proficiency assessments

	Rested	After 12 hours of work
SR	10,76±0,88	10,64±0,64
SV	0,45±0,09	0,43±0,07
VO2	44,90±6,06	47,43±8,55*
TIRO-P	86,28±23,94	73,06±42,44
TIRO-T	15,81±2,97	15,58±3,14
STR-P	62,78±14,00	64,78±18,62

| STR-C | 112,44±13,12 | 114,44±10,25 |

*Significant difference (p<0.05);

SR: shuttle-run (sec.);

SV: vertical jump (cm);

VO2: maximum oxygen volume (ml.kg-1.min-1);

TIRO-P: score in the shooting test;

TIRO-T: time in the shooting test (sec.);

STR-P: correct guesses of the meaning of the words

Only the result of the VO_2 max assessment showed a significant difference (p<0.05) between the experimental conditions, being 5.6 per cent higher after the 12-hour night shift.

The evaluation of the acute effects of night shifts (12 hours) on physical fitness (PA), represented by agility, aerobic capacity and muscle power were verified through the tests in this research. In addition to physical capacity, the effect of such labour activity on cognitive components and specific proficiency (shooting test) was also observed. All of these components partially represent the ability of military police officers to fulfil their duties, given that the demands of these tasks involve a minimum of physical and mental fitness and specific ability.

Night work is known to have a negative influence on physiological and cognitive parameters (SANTANA, 2012) and the individual's general performance is reduced in such a situation. The data presented here did not identify such behaviour (reduced PA). One explanation for this behaviour may lie in the tasks normally performed by these professionals during this work shift. In general, most of the activities involve patrolling in a vehicle, activities performed in a seated position, or even events with low physical demands. Thus, these activities do not seem to have been sufficient to produce fatigue that could negatively influence PA.

At the same time, the professionals tested had a good deal of experience in this role (8.2 ± 7.2 years). This previous experience may have led to functional adaptations that reduced the deleterious effects of labour activity on physical, cognitive and specific proficiency components, resulting in post-work values similar to those found after periods of inactivity.

Finally, another difficulty in identifying changes may be related to the ability of the tests used to measure these alterations. Bearing in mind that the decrease in the capacities assessed was expected, but of a small magnitude, the sensitivity of the tests may not have been adequate for such differences to be identified. Another factor may be related to the inexperience of those being assessed in these protocols. Individuals undergoing tests with which they are unfamiliar may show a learning effect during the assessments. Thus, in the second assessment, even under conditions of fatigue, learning (greater familiarisation) of the test led to an improvement in the results, masking the influence of the work shift on the capacities assessed.

Apparently, the 12-hour night shift was not able to influence the physical and cognitive capacity and shooting proficiency of the individuals assessed. However, experimental limitations, such as the inexperience of all those assessed with the experimental protocols and their application on only two occasions (after rest and after work) may have generated a learning effect in the second assessment, which partially influenced the results.

The group represented in this study does not include all of Paraná's military police, since they all belong to the same region (capital and metropolitan area), which in turn has the same climatic characteristics, workload and volume of occurrences. The pioneering nature of the results allows for further studies with larger groups for evaluation, as well as the possibility that security officers could, for example, carry out physical activities after work, whether they are in training or already working, with some indication that their performance has not been impaired.

One of the great struggles found in the Paraná Military Police is to find a way for police officers to carry out regular physical activity, which doesn't happen due to the demand for work, the relative lack of personnel, the work schedule and the pretence that after duty they need to rest and they really do, but a new possibility is opening up for them to carry out their activities based on the responses found in this study.

CHAPTER 3

High-intensity interval exercise and sleep deprivation.

HOFLINGER, Francielle
SENTONE, Rafael Gomes
SOUZA, Ricardo Martins

Performance in high-intensity activities can be influenced by a number of factors, such as the individual's level of fitness, nutritional status, hydration, energy substrate reserves, among others (ROGATTO, 2002). In addition to these, the relationship between sleep and waking time and the quality of sleep can also partially determine the intensity and duration of the effort made (FULLAGAR, 2015) as well as the perceived difficulty of the activity (MACHADO, 2010). Studies have shown that during a maximum or sub-maximal effort, associated with sleep deprivation, individuals report a greater perceived effort (PSE of subjective perception of effort), without, however, any change in the conduct of the task when compared to a control situation (FRIEDMAN, 2014).

A study of 35 Australian firefighters divided into two groups (with sleep restriction and without sleep restriction) and analysing their performance after their activities, indicated that they overestimated the intensity of exercise after periods of sleep deprivation, but showed similar results to those indicated when not deprived of sleep. This behaviour can be explained by the fact that the body remains in a state of latency - alert - decreasing the metabolism to be activated as needed, demonstrating an adaptation to periods without sleep (VINCENT, 2015).

Some studies have linked a short period of sleep or its desynchronisation to weight gain, obesity, diabetes and hypertension, loss of exercise *performance*, as well as an increased mortality rate (GOEL, 2013; SENTONE,

2014). According to Friedman (2014), sleep deprivation is a factor that can cause changes in *performance* and difficulty in accessing energy reserves. The author suggests that changes in sleep can cause interference at a cortical, physiological, perceptual and behavioural level. The author points out that during or after sleep deprivation, participants reported an increase in perceived effort in cognitive vigilance tasks, complex cognitive tasks and cognitive tasks involving physical labour, and that they had a decreased sense of motivation with increased effort and throughout the period of sleep deprivation (FRIEDMAN, 2014).

Souissi et al. (2003) observed that sleep deprivation for 24 hours does not seem to interfere with anaerobic power and muscle strength, but they did observe changes in performance after 36 hours without sleep. Martin (1981) observed an increase in PSE in subjects deprived of sleep for 36 hours, and there seems to be an inverse relationship between sleep deprivation and the volume of physical exercise, which suggests a protective mechanism. Antunes (2008), after reviewing the literature, found that one of the alterations caused by sleep deprivation is an increase in SPE, which in itself is a factor in the reduction and impairment of physical performance, and may represent an element that "masks" the deleterious effects of deprivation. One explanation for this phenomenon is known as the psychobiological model of fatigue. This model demonstrates a relationship between the perception of effort and the development of the task, whereby the more mentally tired the individual is, the greater their perception of effort in the activity performed (SMIRMAUL, 2013; PLYLEY, 1987).

This situation of sleep deprivation and intense physical exertion can be quite common for some individuals, such as military police officers on duty. In addition, some sporting activities and recreational activities such as ultra-marathons, orienteering races and adventure races require maintaining an effort for relatively long periods (a few days), and sleep can be drastically reduced or not realised at all. People who work shifts (doctors, nurses, drivers) and who exercise regularly may decide to do these activities straight after their working hours, which can interfere with their physical performance. According to Antunes (2008) the literature lacks more significant studies in this regard, since it is difficult to find subjects who are subjected to the conditions of the experiments, and there is no standardisation of the experimental protocols.

In order to understand the possibilities of training after individuals have been deprived of sleep without impairing performance, this study sought to identify the influence of sleep deprivation on the performance, physiological indicators of fatigue and PSE of military police officers during and after *high-intensity interval* exercise *(HIIE)*. Bearing in mind that a range of recreational (e.g. physical activity after a period of shift work), competitive (e.g. ultramarathon, adventure race, orienteering race) and work-related (e.g. firefighters, police officers, security guards) activities can be carried out under such conditions, the results discussed here will help professionals responsible for organising sessions involving maximal and submaximal effort to define better strategies for maintaining performance, indicate suitable times for their practice and also how to predict reductions in performance in activities involved in the effort made during work.

As discussed in the description of the military police's training and operational service, physical training is an activity carried out during the training period and during the course of the career, sometimes after the police work itself. Rotenberg et al (2001) point out that night shift work takes its toll on sleep, generating discouragement, weakness and insomnia directly linked to sleep deprivation, tremor, obesity and premature ageing related to physical aspects, as well as lack of control and aggression in the psychological sphere. If we imagine, much more for those who experience this condition of sleep deprivation and night work, that police officers add to these factors the extra load of equipment, weapons and clothing inherent to the job, as well as the very characteristic of police work in dealing with stressful situations, lack of control, danger and aggression, we realise that military police activity carried out at night is potentiated in all its possibilities.

The challenges of sleep deprivation go beyond the period worked, since after it, imagining that the officers will rest, they are faced with a clear day and naturally, although tired and by the nature of life in society, they will carry out their usual activities such as domestic chores and leisure activities. Even when off duty, military police officers continue their activities and sleep deprivation is maximised.

Far beyond the perceived physical aspects, the effects of sleep deprivation can turn its agents into machines that perform tasks, but don't think in order to carry them out. This effect can be found in the studies by Thomas et al (2000), who demonstrated through brain analysis that a night's sleep deprivation decreases brain activity in alertness and cognitive processes, finding in their studies that the biological need for sleep maintains the normal functioning of brain activities and, above all, for work productivity, public safety (with regard to the safety of the people involved in the work, handling of equipment, etc.) and feelings of well-being.

This automation can become a serious problem for public security, given that its agents deal with society and need to be attentive in order to give them a sensitive response.

Giam (1997) found in military personnel from the navy, army and air force that not sleeping for cumulative periods has a more negative effect on mood, motivation, attention, alertness, short-term memory, ability to complete tasks and physical performance. They also conclude that to compensate for prolonged periods of sleep deprivation, 10 to 12 hours of sleep are needed to return to normal. The deleterious effects of sleep deprivation cause disorders in police work that reduce its effectiveness both in the way it deals with incidents (with very high numbers per day) and in the responses given to them.

Public security is a fertile field for study and should not be mitigated by the academic field, but on the contrary, relentlessly pursued for its development, as it is real and present in the lives of Brazilians and in many countries around the world. Biological clarifications have the potential to improve military police training.

High Intensity Interval Training (HIIT)

Because it involves short training sessions, interval exercise seems to be one of the most practical ways of promoting health and fitness benefits. Although it has been extensively researched in the last 10 years, it has already been practised by runners since the 1930s and 1940s (DANIELS; SCARDINA, 1984).

The method consists of performing short bursts of a few seconds at moderate or high intensities in the same exercise, separated by recovery periods of low intensity (GILLEN; GIBALA, 2013), which leads to physiological changes, such as oxidative capacity and glycaemic control, in less time than continuous long-term exercise (GILLEN et al., 2014).

One of the most investigated protocols in the literature is the Wingate protocol, created in the 1970s. The test consists of 30-second maximal shots on a stationary bicycle, with 4 minutes of active recovery, with the aim of measuring anaerobic power (GILLEN; GIBALA, 2014). However, the effort required in this protocol is barely tolerable for non-athletes. For this reason, the number of studies using interval exercise at submaximal intensities has increased, investigating acute and chronic adaptations (LUCAS et al., 2009).

In this way, other interval exercise protocol models may be more viable and still be just as efficient in terms of time and gains compared to the Wingate protocol (GILLEN; GIBALA, 2013).

Although its optimal prescription has yet to be fully clarified, growing evidence suggests that training with short bouts of relatively intense exercise can be an effective strategy for improving fitness and health.

A case study

This study assessed 12 apparently healthy young subjects (33.2±5.9

years; 1.7±0.1m; 75.8±14.6kg; 7 men and 5 women). All were informed of the experimental procedures and signed an informed consent form accepting the invitation to take part in the experiment. Subjects who reported any type of musculoskeletal or cardiorespiratory problem, as well as recent injuries or surgeries that could interfere with the performance of the activity, were excluded. All the military police officers carried out operational public safety activities in their professional lives.

Procedures

After receiving the necessary information about the procedures and carrying out the anthropometric assessments, the participants underwent 4 tests in different sessions, with a minimum interval of 48 hours between them. Initially (session 1) the subjects filled in the IPAQ questionnaire (reduced, PARDINI, 2001) in an attempt to delineate the quality of life of the agents , the Pittsburgh Sleep Quality Index (PSQI) questionnaire (BERTOLAZI, 2008) to assess the quality and disturbances of their sleep over a period of one month, and finally a chronotype test (HORNE and OSTBERG, 1976) was carried out to delineate which of them had predominantly morning, afternoon or indifferent characteristics.

In the same session, the maximum load (MAX) supported by each individual was determined, for subsequent test delimitations, on a bicycle ergometer with electromagnetic resistance that had the intensity of the load calibrated with a scale of arbitrary units for the stress tests. The officers began the test with a zero load in the first stage, with a rotation of 40 to 45 RPM. After the first stage, the load underwent unit increments and increases of 5 RPM every minute. The test was terminated when the subjects were unable to maintain the pre-established RPM with the respective load.

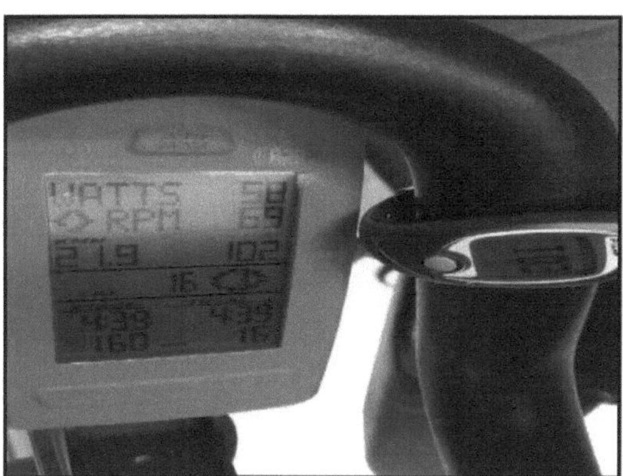

Figure 10. Cycle ergometer screen during collection. Source: the authors. 2016.

The second session was used as an introduction to the test. The interval exercise was performed with 10 8-second shots, interspersed with a 12-second active recovery in free rotation, determined by the participant, with a total duration of 3min20s. Pedal resistance was set at 75% of the load determined in the test described above (MAX).

In the third and fourth sessions, the aforementioned interval test protocol was applied in two different contexts: immediately after the subjects had been sleep deprived (PRI) for a period of ~24 hours and after a period of rest (DES, ordinary day), all in the morning after the subjects had worked or rested. In the period leading up to the sleep deprivation test, participants were instructed not to nap or consume any substance that could stimulate them such as caffeine, alcohol or large amounts of sugar during the day leading up to the assessment. The order of the sessions (PRI- DES or DES-PRI) was randomised according to the performance obtained in the initial test (session 1), where the 1st, 3rd, 5th, 7th, 9th and 11th results were allocated to the PRI-DES order and the 2nd, 4th, 6th, 8th, 10th and 12th results to the DES-PRI order.

During the tests in sessions 3 and 4, the levels of Subjective Perception of Effort (PSE) were recorded at the end of the 5th and 10th shots using the OMNI-Cycling scale (SILVA, 2011).

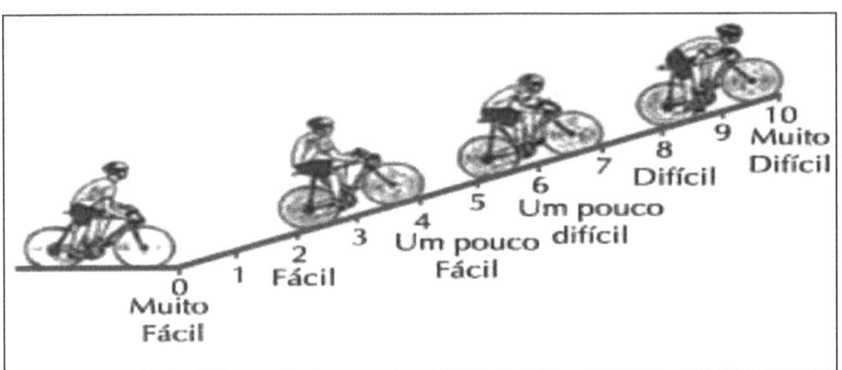

Figure 11. OMNI scale for assessing Subjective Perception of Effort for adults during the cycle ergometer test. Adapted to Portuguese. Source: Silva, 2011.

PSE is a way of prescribing and monitoring training loads in different physical tasks, i.e. responding to the intensity of the exercise by quantifying the sensation of effort generated by the subject. According to Nakamura et al (2010), there is evidence available to suggest that the PSE method, in a training session, is a low-cost, simple and reliable strategy for monitoring training loads, as well as demonstrating that in various studies, internal indicators of exercise intensity (oxygen consumption, heart rate and lactate concentration) show a strong relationship with PSE behaviour.

Blood lactate (BLA) was measured using a lactimeter (Accutrend Lactate, ROCHE) immediately before and 1 minute after the end of all the test runs. The parameters of effort (% of maximum heart rate - HR; max HR = 208 - 0.7 x age) and work done (maximum pedal rotation per minute - RPM) in each of the runs were provided by a frequency meter (FS1, Polar) and the bike's own dashboard, respectively. Throughout the tests (sessions 3 and 4) the individuals were verbally encouraged by the assessors, trying to positively influence the maintenance of the high intensity of the intended effort.

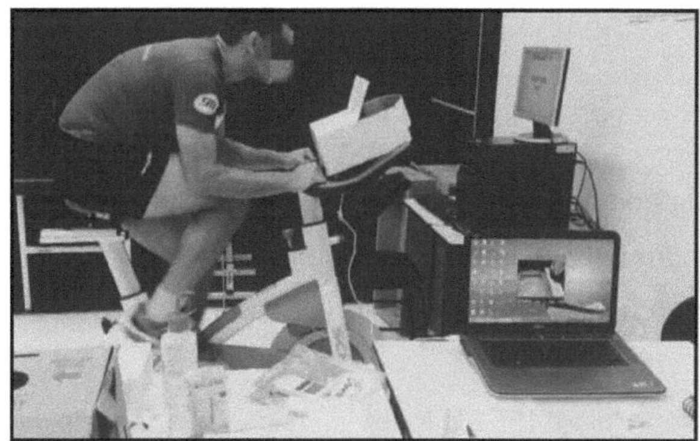

Figure 12. Data collection during one of the tests. Source: the authors. 2016.

Statistical analysis

A normality test was applied to the data (Shapiro-Willks). As the data did not show a normal distribution, non-parametric analyses were used. To check whether there was an influence of sleep deprivation on HR and RPM in all the shots taken, a Friedman test was applied. A post-hoc test was applied to identify where these differences occurred. A Wilcoxon test was applied to identify differences between LAC and PSE between the two collections. All tests were applied with a significance level of $p < 0.05$. All procedures were applied using SPSS 20 software (IBM, USA).

CHAPTER 4

Results

All the experimental procedures were carried out without any adverse events. The subjects only reported the expected discomfort of carrying out the procedure. All values are represented as their mean and standard deviation (mean; ±standard deviation).

Individuals who reported doing 150 or more minutes of moderate or vigorous physical activity per week were classified as "active", those who did between 11 and 149 minutes as "insufficiently active" and those who did less than 10 minutes continuously during the week as "sedentary". Sleep quality was assessed using the sum of the seven components that make up the PSQI questionnaire (subjective sleep quality; sleep latency; sleep duration; habitual sleep efficiency; sleep disturbances; use of sleep medication; dysfunction during the day), classified as "good", "bad" and "presence of sleep disturbance". No individuals with a typical morning or afternoon chronotype were identified, who could therefore have greater or lesser difficulty with these experimental procedures. Table 1 summarises the data on physical activity level (IPAQ), sleep quality index (PSQI) and chronotype.

Table 1 - Participants' level of physical activity (IPAQ), level of sleep quality (PSQI) and chronotype.

IPAQ			PSQI	CHRONOTYPE		
Active	Ins-active	Good	Bad	Mod-Mat	Indif.	Mod-Vesp
3	9	4	8	1	8	3

Ins-Active: Insufficiently active; Mod-Mat: moderately morning; Indif: Indifferent;
Mod-Vesp: Moderately afternoon

Table 2 shows the results of the variables relating to the perception of effort (PSE) and physiological stress (LAC) of the participants in this experiment, in the conditions with (PRI) and rested (DES) sleep deprivation.

Table 2 - Perceived exertion (PSE) and blood lactate concentration (LAC) during the test with (PRI) and rested (DES) sleep deprivation.

	PRI	DES
PSE-5	5,0±0,8	4,9±1,3
PSE-10	7,7±1,3*	7,0±1,7*
LAC-I	1,7±0,6	1,6±0,8
LAC-II	8,3±2,8**	9,2±3,3**

PSE-5: subjective perception of effort after the 5th maximum shot;
PSE-10: subjective perception of effort after the 10th maximum shot;
LAC-I: blood lactate concentration immediately before the start of the test;
LAC-II: blood lactate concentration T after the end of the test;
* difference compared to PSE-5 ($p<0.05$);
** difference compared to LAC-I ($p<0.05$).

Table 3 shows the results of the variables relating to maximum heart rate (HR) and maximum speed (RPM) for each of the shots performed in the two experimental conditions.

Table 3 - Percentage of maximum heart rate (HR) and maximum speed (RPM) in each of the shots (1 to 10) during the test with (PRI) and without (SEM) sleep deprivation.

	PRI	DES		PRI	DES
FC-1	76,5±5,8	72,3±8,3	**RPM-1**	169,1 ±22,3	168,1 ±32,7
FC-2	82,7±7,0	78,5±7,7	**RPM-2**	168,5±17,7	169,6±27,8
FC-3	86,2±7,4	83,1 ±9,6	**RPM-3**	165,8±17,6	166,5±27,8
FC-4	88,5±7,5	85,7±8,9	**RPM-4**	162,8±16,8	160,6±25,0
FC-5	89,6±6,9	88,5±7,5	**RPM-5**	157,8±17,1	157,2±22,9
FC-6	90,9±6,5	89,7±7,5	**RPM-6**	156,0±15,9	154,0±22,2
FC-7	92,2±6,1	91,7±7,6	**RPM-7**	153,4±14,8	152,4±20,3
FC-8	92,7±6,0	91,2±8,5	**RPM-8**	151,3±14,0	152,8±19,0
FC-9	93,6±5,6	92,1 ±8,1	**RPM-9**	152,2±16,6	153,5±18,0
FC-10	93,9±5,5	92,5±7,9	**RPM-10**	153,5±16,4	152,1±17,9

CHAPTER 5

Discussion

The aim is to understand the effects of sleep deprivation on the ability of individuals to perform high-intensity interval activity immediately after periods of 24 hours of sleep deprivation on average. Bearing in mind that various activities can be carried out in such a context of sleep deprivation, such as activities carried out by military police, army, navy, aeronautics and on-call doctors, it is important to identify how much the quality of service of these workers could be influenced by such a condition.

Vaara and Vicent (2009, 2015) investigated the effects on the performance of 20 young cadets and 32 firefighters, respectively, due to sleep deprivation for periods of 2 to 60 hours and 4 hours of sleep, respectively. The authors concluded that the groups that were deprived of sleep were less active, had an increase in blood flow through the vagus as evidenced by a decrease in heart rate, as well as a decrease in body temperature during sleep deprivation.

However, none of the previous studies looked at the interference of sleep deprivation on physiological and perceptual effort variables, and they were concerned with controlling the influence of chronotype, sleep quality and the volume of physical activity carried out by the individuals. Knowing that the level of physical fitness, quality of sleep and circadian rhythm characteristics can influence the development of the proposed task in such experimental conditions, we believe it is essential to control these variables.

As for chronotype, none of the participants were classified as typically morning or afternoon (8 indifferent, 1 moderately morning and 3 moderately afternoon), reducing the possibility that chronotype could interfere with performance, especially in the sleep deprivation condition (PRI). The subjects also showed a tendency to have poor sleep quality, which was reported by 8 of the 12 assessed. The amount of weekly physical activity, which could influence the individuals' level of physical fitness, was insufficient (9 out of 12) according to the classification proposed by Matsudo et al. (2002) and the CDC (2002). Therefore, it is possible to believe that the group had a certain homogeneity in terms of its characteristics, and that these characteristics had little influence on the outcome of the task.

The proposed activity was clearly carried out at an intensity considered high in both conditions, given the perceived exertion (PSE) reported at the end of the test (PRI 7.7±1.3 and DES 7.0±1.7). However, no differences were identified (p>0.05) between the experimental conditions. The other indicator of the effort made, blood lactate, also showed values considered adequate to represent high-intensity activity (PRI 8.3±2.8 and DES 9.2±3.3), and likewise showed no influence (p>0.05) from the experimental condition. It can therefore be concluded that the activity chosen was suitable for the purpose of the study and that the experimental conditions (DES and PRI) did not influence these variables.

In both experimental sessions (3 and 4) the activity had similar characteristics (p>0.05) in terms of the work (RPM) and percentage of maximum heart rate (HR) achieved. It was clear that the individuals were motivated to perform each of the 10 proposed shots at maximum intensity, and it was possible to identify that from the second (PRI) and third (DES) shot the activity could already be considered high intensity (>80% max HR). At the end of the test, in both experimental conditions, the maximum frequency reached exceeded the predicted 90% (HRmax = 208 - 0.7 x age). Previous studies have found that in similar protocols an effort very close to that identified in this study is expected.

Mueller et. al. and Jung (2015, 2014) analysed the effects of high-intensity training (HIT) and, among the findings, found that the heart rate after such training is higher.

Bearing in mind that the activity produced a physical demand close to maximum, and that all the parameters used to verify these factors did not change between the experimental conditions (DES and PRI), some hypotheses were raised to explain these results.

Although the sleep deprivation found was significant (~24h), the participating individuals are reasonably adapted to this condition. When the interview was carried out during the sample selection phase, the individuals reported that they experience a period of sleep deprivation approximately twice a week. However, the deprivation is not always so long, and is usually around 12-14 hours and always at night (usually between 5pm and 5am the next day). We believe that even this reduced deprivation compared to that used in the present study, which occurs sporadically, may have provided a condition in the individuals that allowed for better physiological and perceptual assimilation of the effort made in our experiment.

Souissi et al. (2003) observed that individuals who performed the Wingate test associated with sleep deprivation for 24 hours also had no change in performance, as found in the present study.

In addition to this relative adaptation to the condition of deprivation that the individuals in this study are suspected to have gone through, the activities carried out during the period in which they are awake at dawn require little physical effort and thus add little fatigue to the period of deprivation. The subjects were patrolling in motorised vehicles, with a very low frequency of physical activity. Therefore, although sleep deprivation probably caused an increase in tiredness at the end of the working day (not measured), the magnitude of this tiredness may not have been large enough to interfere with test performance and the physiological variables measured.

Thus, the results of this study suggest that relatively long periods of sleep deprivation (~24 hours) do not produce alterations in the work performance capacity of subjects who are partially adapted to this condition. Even if it were necessary to exert close to maximum effort during this labour activity, it is believed that performance would not be affected, thus guaranteeing a satisfactory quality of service. However, it is not possible to predict how people who are not adapted to such conditions would respond to the same experimental protocol, or even whether people who are adapted but who exert substantially more physical effort during the deprivation period would show the same results. Future studies are suggested to verify these conditions.

CHAPTER 6

AUTHOR'S NOTE

The questions posed in this work reflect some of the anguish regarding the answers that have not been found throughout my career. One could walk along the same path as the occult, following in the footsteps of an institutional culture that deserves to be explored in depth in all its areas of activity and which is afflicted, as in this case, by the effects of police work on the physiological order.

Physical training is part of a military policeman's life and we are required throughout our career to always be in top condition. Some memories from my training days reveal that physical training after nights on duty, whether in curricular classes or through the training itself, had a heavy air of execution and there were always suggestions among the students that the bad nights were masking and subduing our real performance, which was actually clarified, at least in part, through the discussions proposed here.

On other occasions, now that I've graduated, after hours of dealing with police reports, arrests, referrals to police stations, police operations and various activities, I've come across the lightness with which police officers treat the practice of physical education, the cult of body health. Routinely, abstaining from exercise is accompanied by eating *fast food, which alone* would be worth another book and discussion. The unveiling really does seem to be incorporated into the military police institutional culture and does not seem to significantly affect aspects of physical performance or high-intensity training, even if the perceptions are much deeper with regard to tiredness, which now seems to us to be of a psychological nature.

Our aim at the end of this book is to provide some answers and clarifications, but much more to provoke new research and publicity, because through it we can be seen as people clad in the mantle of hierarchy and discipline that imbues us with the ability to save lives, as well as our own health, often due to the sleep deprivation of night-time vigils on the streets and the heavy equipment that is needed to carry out our work.

Physical education deserves to be thought of in the Military Police as ergonomic, aimed at the well-being of its officers and promoting better working conditions through cultivation, using our organisational processes to inculcate the practice of physical activity as healthy and beneficial habits for the individual and society. A profession that has high rates of heart disease, suicides, deaths on duty and lower life expectancy among its officers compared to the general population needs to break with this decline in life.

Our goals are greater, noble, and we will not let ourselves be overwhelmed by the perils that naturally beset us, but we will carry them through, solidifying ourselves more and more through the distinguished work we do on a daily basis. Forward PMPR! Howl! Howl! Howl!

ANNEX
Word Reading: Record Sheet

Instructions: Now we have more written words here. I'd like you to read these words out loud to me as quickly as you can. Start at the beginning of the first column, when you've finished go to the second, then the third and finally the last. If you make a mistake, correct it and continue. After I say "Now", start. Understood? Then pay attention: Now!

Time: Give the start signal at the same time as you start the stopwatch. The time limit is 120 seconds. Say: "Enough, you can stop" when the time limit is up.

Quotation: Mark correct answers with A tick, incorrect answers with a cross **X** and spontaneous corrections with a C mark. Record the time the subject took to complete the task, or 120 seconds.

1 BLUE	29 GREEN	57 ROSA	85 GREEN
2 GREEN	30 BLUE	58 GREEN	86 GREY
3 PINK	31 ROSA	59 BLUE	87 ROSA
4 GREY	32 BLUE	60 GREY	88 GREY
5 GREEN	33 GREY	61 ROSA	89 BLUE

6 BLUE	34 ROSA	62 GREY	90 GREY
7 PINK	35 GREEN	63 BLUE	91 GREEN
8 GREY	36 GREY	64 GREY	92 ROSA
9 PINK	37 GREEN	65 ROSA	93 GREEN
10 BLUE	38 BLUE	66 BLUE	94 ROSA
11 PINK	39 ROSA	67 ROSA	95 BLUE
12 GREY	40 GREY	68 GREY	96 GREEN
13 BLUE	41 GREEN	69 BLUE	97 GREY
14 GREY	42 PINK	70 GREEN	98 BLUE
15 PINK	43 BLUE	71 GREY	99 GREEN
16 BLUE	44 GREEN	72 BLUE	100 PINK
17 GREEN	45 ROSA	73 GREY	101 GREEN
18 GREY	46 GREEN	74 BLUE	102 GREY
19 GREEN	47 BLUE	75 ROSA	103 GREEN
20 GREY	48 GREY	76 GREEN	104 BLUE
21 PINK	49 GREEN	77 BLUE	105 GREY
22 BLUE	50 PINK	78 GREEN	106 BLUE
23 ROSA	51 GREY	79 BLUE	107 GREEN
24 GREY	52 BLUE	80 GREEN	108 ROSA
25 PINK	53 GREY	81 ROSA	109 BLUE
26 GREY	54 ROSA	82 GREEN	110 GREEN
27 GREEN	55 GREY	83 GREY	111 ROSA
28 GREY	56 GREEN	84 ROSA	112 BLUE

Time = __ s

Total Responses =

Incorrect (X) = _

Correct (^) = _

Colour Naming: Record Sheet

Training, Instructions: Now we're going to do a different task [present the Reading and Naming Training Sheet]. Instead of reading the words, I'd like you to tell me the **colour of the ink** they're printed in. Tick the answers on the front page. [Move on to the test itself after making sure that the subject has understood what needs to be done. If necessary, repeat the training and explain that this task requires concentration. Try to motivate the subject to do the task well, but without creating fear of failure].

Instructions: Let's do the same with more words. I'd like you to tell me the

colour of the ink the words are printed in, as quickly as you can. Start at the beginning of the 1st column, when you've finished move on to the 2nd, and so on. If you make a mistake, correct it and continue. As before, you don't start until I give the signal (say "now"). Is that clear? Attention: Now!

Time: Give the start signal at the same time as you start the stopwatch. The time limit is 120 seconds. **Quotation:** Mark correct answers with A tick, incorrect answers with a cross, and spontaneous corrections with a C. Mark the time it took you to complete the task, or 120 seconds. Mark the time it took you to complete the task, or 120 seconds.

1 PINK	29 BLUE	57 BLUE	85 GREY
2 BLUE	30 GREY	58 GREY	86 ROSA
3 GREEN	**31 GREEN**	**59 ROSA**	**87 GREEN**
4 BLUE	32 ROSA	60 GREEN	88 BLUE
5 PINK	33 BLUE	61 GREY	89 GREY
6 GREY	34 GREEN	62 ROSA	90 GREEN
7 BLUE.	**35 BLUE**	**63 GREEN**	**91 ROSA**
8 PINK	36 GREEN	64 BLUE	92 GREY
9 GREY	37 ROSA	65 GREEN	93 BLUE
10 GREEN	38 GREY	66 GREY	94 GREEN
11 BLUE	**39 BLUE**	**67 BLUE**	**95 ROSA**
12 PINK	40 PINK	68 GREEN	96 GREY
13 GREY	41 BLUE	69 ROSA	97 ROSA
14 BLUE_	42 GREY	70 BLUE	98 GREEN
15 GREEN	**43 ROSA**	**71 ROSA**	**99 ROSA**
16 PINK	44 GREY	72 GREEN	100 BLUE
17 GREY_	45 BLUE	73 BLUE	101 PINK
18 GREEN	46 ROSA	74 GREY	102 BLUE
19 BLUE_	**47 GREEN**	**75 GREEN**	**103 GREY**
20 PINK	48 BLUE	76 BLUE	104 GREEN
21 GREY	49 GREY	77 ROSA	105 ROSA
22 GREEN	50 GREEN	78 GREY	106 GREY
23 BLUE	**51 ROSA**	**79 GREEN**	**107 BLUE**
24 GREEN	52 GREY	80 ROSA	108 GREY
25 GREY	53 GREEN	81 GREY	109 ROSA
26 BLUE_	54 GREY	82 BLUE	110 BLUE
27 GREY	**55 BLUE**	**83 GREEN**	**111 GREEN**
28 ROSA	56 ROSA	84 BLUE	112 GREY

Time =s

Total Responses = -

Incorrect (X) = -

Correct ( ) = -----

REFERENCES

1. ANTUNES, H. K. M. et al. Sleep deprivation and physical exercise. **Rev. bras. med. esporte,** v. 14, n. 1, p. 51-56, jan./feb. 2008.

2. BERRIA J., DERONCO L. S. E., BEVILACQUA L. A. Motor fitness and work capacity of military police officers from the Special Operations Battalion. **Salusvita,** Bauru, v. 31, n. 2, 89-104. 2011.

3. BERTOLAZI, A. N. **Translation, cultural adaptation and validation of two sleep assessment instruments:** Epworth Sleepiness Scale and Pittsburgh Sleep Quality Index. 2008.

4. BONNEAU, J., BROWN, J. TR-03-97. Physical Ability, Fitness and Police Work. **Journal of Clinical Forensic Medicine,** v. 2, pp. 157-164, 1995.

5. BRAZIL. **Constitution of the Federative Republic of Brazil.** 5 October 1988.

6. BRAZIL. Decree No. 3.182, of 23 September 1999. Regulates Law No. 9.786, of 8 February 1999, which provides for **teaching in the Brazilian Army and makes other provisions.**

7. BRETÃS, M. L.; ROSEMBERG, A. A história da polícia no Brasil: balanço e perespectivas. **Topoi,** v. 14, n. 26, jan./juL, 162-173. 2013.

8. CARLI A. G., OLIVEIRA R. S. Effect of the use of personal protective equipment and respiratory equipment on the VO2 max of members of the

16th Fire Brigade of the Military Police of the State of São Paulo.

Revista Brasileira de Prescrição e Fisiologia do Exercício, São Paulo, v. 6, n. 35, p. 501-505, Sep/Oct 2012.

9. CASTRO, S. L. et. al. **Stroop Neuropsychological Test in Portuguese.** Speech Laboratory of the Faculty of Psychology of the University of Porto. 2009.

10. COLLINGWOOD, T., HOFFMAN, R., SMITH, J. Underlying physical fitness factors for performing police officer tasks. **Police Chief,** pp. 32-37, 2004.

11. COSTA, G. A. Cardiorespiratory Fitness of Schoolchildren at CAIC in Taguatinga. Shuttle Run Test. Catholic University (LEGER and LAMBERT, 1982). 2010.

12. COSTA, M., et al. Stress: diagnosis of military police officers in a Brazilian city. **Rev Panam Salud Publica.** 21 (4). 2007.

13. DANIELS, J.; SCARDINA, N. **Interval training and performance.** Sports Medicine, Auckland, n. 1, p. 327-34, 1984.

14. DENNING D. L. **Applying the Hogan model of physical performance of occupational tasks.** Toronto: Paper presented at the American Psychological Association Convention, 1984

15. DERENUSSON, F. C., JABLONSKI, B. Under crossfire: the impact of military police work on the police officer's family. **Aletheia.** Canoas, n. 32, Aug. 2010.

16. DERRICK L. G., HENN H. R., MALONE G. H. The infiuence of body armour cov- erage and weight on the performance of the marine while performing certain simulated combat type tasks. **Naval Field Medical Research Laboratory.** 13(29); 1-9. 1963.

17. ESTRELA, A. L. **Measures and Evaluation in Physical Education.** Pontifical Catholic University of Rio Grande do Sul (ASTRAND BANK). 2010.

18. FAHEY T. D. **Bases of strength training for men and women.** Artmed. 8ª ed. Rio Grande do Sul, p. 11. 2014.

19. FARENHOLTZ D, RHODES E. C. Police officer physical abilities study. Vancouver: **Justice Institute of British Columbia,** November 1986

20. FRAGA, C. K. Peculiarities of military police work. **Virtual magazine texts & contexts.** No. 6, December 2006.

21. FRIEDMAN, M. E. **The effects of sleep loss on capacity and effort.** Sleep Science 7. P. 2013-224. 2014.

22. FULLAGAR, H. H. K et al. Sleep and athletic performance: the effects of sleep loss on exercise performance, and physiological and cognitive responses to exercise. **Sports medicine,** v. 45, n. 2, p. 161-186, 2015.

23. GIL, A. C. **Como Elaborar Projetos de Pesquisa.** 4. Ed. São Paulo: Atlas S. A. 2002.

24. GIAM G. C. **Effects of sleep deprivation with reference to military**

operations. Annals of the Academy of Medicine. Singapore, 26(1), 88:93. 1997.

25. GOEL, N. et al. Circadian rhythms, sleep deprivation, and human performance. **Progress in molecular biology and translational Science,** v. 119, p. 155, 201.

26. GONÇALVES, S. M. P. **Bem-estar no trabalho com contexto policial: O contribuição dos valores e das práticas organizacionais.** Doctoral Thesis. University Institute of Lisbon. 2011.

27. GRUBER G. P. et al. Physical fitness standards for the Calgary police Service. **Calgary: Police Service, Project** no. 83, Report 3, 1983.

28. GILLEN, J. B. et al. **Three Minutes of All-Out Intermittent Exercise per Week Increases Skeletal Muscle Oxidative Capacity and Improves Cardiometabolic Health,** PLOS ONE, year 14, n. 9, p. 1-9, nov. 2014.

29. GILLEN, Jenna B ; GIBALA Martin **J.Is high-intensity interval training a time-efficient exercise strategy to improve health and fitness?,** NRC Research Press Canada, year 11, n. 39, p. 409-412, sep. 2013

30. GUIMARÃES, L. A. M. et al. Burnout syndrome and quality of life of military and civilian police officers. Revista Sul Americana de Psicologia, v. 2, n. 1, jan./jun. 2014.

31. HAISMAN M. F., CROTTY J.: **Problems associated with body armour.** Paper at the 11 th Commonwealth Defence Conference on Operational Clothing and Combat Equipment, 1975. In: Handbook on Clothing: Biomedical Effects of Military Clothing and Equipment Systems, Ed 2. Edited by Goldmann R, Kampmann B. Soesterberg, Netherlands, TNO,

Institute of Perception, 2007.

32. HENDERSON J. **Personal communication.** Royal Ulter Constabulary, 1995.

33. HOFFMAN, R., COLLINGWOOD, T. Fit for Duty: the officer's Guide to Total Fitness 2nd edition. Champaign, IL. **Human Kinetcs Publishing.** 2005.

34. HOLEWIJN, M., LOTENS, W. A. The influence of backpack design on physical performance. **Ergonomics.** 35(2); 149-157. 1992.

35. HORNE, J. A., OSTBERG, O. A self-assessment questionnaire to determine morningness-eveningness in human circadian rhythms. **International journal of chronobiology,** v. 4, n. 2, p. 97-110, 1975.

36. JESUS, G. M., MOTA, N. M., JESUS, E. F. A. Cardiovascular risk in military police officers from a large city in northeastern Brazil. **Rev Bras de Ciências do Esport,** v. 36, n. 3, jul./set, 692-699. 2014.

37. JUNG, M. E., BOURNE, J. E., Little, J. P. Where does HIT fit? An examination of the affective response to high-intervals in comparison to continous moderate and continous vigorous intensity exercise in the exercise intensity-affect continuum. **Pios One.** 9(12),   2014. DOI 10.1371/journal.pone.0114541.

38. LEGER, L., LAMBERT, J. A maximal multistage 20m run test to predict VO2 max. **European Journal of Applied Physiology,** v.49, p.01-12, 1982.

39. LEOPOLD R. S., DERRICK L. G. The effect of wearing body armour of different designs, materials and weights on the performance of the marine.

Naval Field Medical Research Laboratory. 12(12), 30. 1962.

40. LEOPOLD R. S., DERRICK L. G. The effect of wearing body armour of different designs, materials and weights in conjunction with two designs of packs and suspenders on the performance of the marine. **Naval Field Medical Research Laboratory,** 13(18). 1963.

41. LOTENS W. A. Selection of body armour for the Royal Dutch Army I: Fuctional Characteristics. **Report Institute for Perception,** IZF 1981-15, 1981.

42. LUCAS, Ricardo Dantas, et al. **Physiological responses during continuous and intermittent exercise: implications for the assessment and prescription of aerobic training.** Motriz, Rio Claro, v.15, n.4, p.810-820, October-December 2009.

43. MACHADO, J. R. M. et al. Subjective perception of effort as load control in indoor cycling classes. **Brazilian Journal of Sports and Exercise Research,** v. 1 (1), p. 42-47, 2010.

44. MARTIN, Bruce J. Effect of sleep deprivation on tolerance of prolonged exercise. **European journal of applied physiology and occupational physiology,** v. 47, n. 4, p. 345-354, 1981.

45. MATSUDO, Victor et al. Promotion of physical activity in a developing country: the Agita Sao Paulo experience. **Public health nutrition,** v. 5, n. 1a, p. 253-261, 2002.

46. MELLO C. M. A., NUMMER F. V. **Policial Militar: uma profissão de risco.** 29ª Reunião Brasileira de Antropologia. Natal/RN. 2014. www.29rba.abant.org.br.resources/anais/1/1401917965_ARQUIVO_Artig

oRB A2014CesareFernanda.pdf. Accessed on 23 March 2017.

47. MINAYO, M. C. S., ASSIS, S. G., OLIVEIRA R. V. C. Impacto das atividades profissionais na saúde física e mental dos policiais civis e militares do Rio de Janeiro. **Ciênc. Saúde coleitva.** Rio de Janeiro, v. 16, n. 4, jan./abr. 2011.

48. MULLER, S. M. et.al. High-intensity interval training with vibration as rest intervals attenuates fibre atrophy and prevents decreases in anaerobic performance. **Pios One.** 10(2), 2015. DOI 10.1371/journal.pone.0116764.

49. NAKAMURA, Fabio Yuzo; MOREIRA, Alexandre; AOKI, Marcelo Saldanha. **Monitoring training load: is subjective perception of session effort a reliable method?-doi:** 10.4025/reveducfis. v21i1. 6713. Revista da Educação Física/UEM, v. 21, n. 1, p. 1-11,2010.

50. NETO, P. M. Policiamento comunitário e prevenção do crime: a visão dos coronéis da polícia militar. **São Paulo in Perspective.** 18(1), 103-110. 2004.

51. OLIVEIRA, P. L. M., BARDAGI, M. P. Stress and career commitment in military police officers. **Boletim de psicologia.** São Paulo, v. 59, n. 131.2009.

52. OSBORN G. D. Validation physical agility tests. **The Police Chief,** p. 43-46. 1976.

53. PARANÁ. State Law No. 17.590, of 12 June 2013, Amends the provisions it specifies of Law No. 13.283, of 25 October 2001, amended by Law No. 13.385, of 21 December 2001, which integrates the higher education entities it mentions into a single autarchy, called the **State University of**

Paraná - UNESPAR, and adopts other measures.

54. PARANÁ. PMPR. Decree no. 4212 - 03/02/2009. Published in Official Gazette no. 7903 of 03/02/2009. Summary: Regulates, within the scope of the State of Paraná, the provisions of Article 67 of Federal Law 9394/1996, as amended by Federal Law 11.301/2006.

55. PARANÁ. PMPR. Guideline No. 004/2015. **Selective or differentiated use of force.** 2015.

56. PARANÁ. PMPR. State Law No. 1,943 of 23 June 1954. Official State Gazette No. 098, of 5 July 1954. **Paraná Military Police Code.**

57. PARANÁ. PMPR. Published in the addendum to BG no. 037, of 25 February 2008, CG Ordinance no. 236, of 26 February 2008.

58. PARDINI, R. et al. Validation of the International Physical Activity Questionnaire (IPAQ-version 6): a pilot study in young Brazilian adults.**Rev. Bras. Ciên. e Mov. Brasília v,** v. 9, n. 3, p. 39-44, 2001.

59. PEOPLES, G. et. al. **The effect af a tiered body armour system on soldier physical mobility.** University of Wollongong, Australia. 2010.

60. PLYLEY, M. J. et al. **Sleep deprivation and cardiorespiratory function.** Influence of intermittent submaximal exercise. European Journal of applied Physiology.

61. RICCIARDI R., DEUSTER P., TALBOT L. Metabolic demands of body armour on physical performance in simulated conditions. **Mil Med,** 173, 817-24. 2008.

62. ROGATTO, G. P., LUCIANO, E. Effects of intense physical training on carbohydrate metabolism. **Physical activity and health.** V. 6, n. 2, 2002, p. 39-46.

63. ROTENBERG, L. et al. Gender and night work: sleep, daily life and the experiences of those who exchange night for day. Rio de Janeiro, **Cad. Saúde Pública,** v. 17, n. 3, mai./jun. 2001.

64. SALLES, P. G. et. al. Validity and Reliability of the Sargent Jump Test in Assessing the Explosive Strength of Football Players. **Brazilian Journal of Health Sciences.** 2010.

65. SANTANA, S. L., SABINO, A. D. V. **Military Police Stress: psychosocial effects.** Três Lagoas Integrated Colleges. Minas Gerais. 2012.

66. SARDINHA, A., et. al. Translation and cross-cultural adaptation of the Habitual Physical Activity Questionnaire. **Journal of Clinical Psychology.** Rio de Janeiro. 2009.

67. SENTONE, R. G.; SOUZA, R. M. **Physical, cognitive and shooting proficiency effects after night duty for military police officers in the State of Paraná.** In: XII Latin American International Scientific Congress and XII Brazilian Scientific Congress of FIEP 'Prof. Dr Manoel José Gomes Tubino', 2015, Foz do Iguaçu. FIEP Bulletin. Foz do Iguaçu: FIEP, 2015. v. 85. p. 24-24.

68. SILVA, A. C. et al. OMNI and Borg scales for the prescription of cycle ergometer exercise. **Revista Brasileira de Cineantropometria & Desempenho Humano,** v. 13, n. 2, p. 117-123, 2011.

69.SMIRMAUL, B. P. C. et al. The psychobiological model: a new explanation to intensity regulation and (in) tolerance in endurance exercise.**Revista Brasileira de Educação Física e Esporte,** v. 27, n. 2, p. 333-340, 2013.

70.SOAR, C. et. al. Waist-hip ratio and waist circumference associated with body mass index in a study of schoolchildren. **Cad. Saúde Pública.** Rio de Janeiro, 20(6), 1609-1616, Nov./Dec. 2004.

71.SOUISSI, Nizar et al. Effects of one nighfs sleep deprivation on anaerobic performance the following day. **European Journal of Applied Physiology,** v. 89, n. 3-4, p. 359-366, 2003.

72.SOUZA E. S., HALTMANN H. Meninos e meninas: expectativas corporais e implicações na educação física escolar.Cadernos **Cedes,** ano XIX, n° 48. 1999.

73.SOUZA M. G., MOMESSO C. M., ROMANHOLO R. A. Stress and physical conditioning: the influence on the performance of police officers from the special operations group of Caocal/RO. **Rev. Bras de Prescrição e Fisio do Exerc.** São Paulo, v. 5, n. 25, jan./feb., p. 21-26. 2011.

74.SPAULDING D. Skills, drills & standards. Combative firearms drills designed to test the shooter's essential skills. **Law Officer Magazine,** apr, p. 47-49. 2013.

75.STORANI P. **Perceptual-motor training to improve police shooting performance in armed confrontations in high-risk areas.** Monograph. Gama Filho University. Rio de Janeiro. 2000. www.comunidadesegura.org.br/files/treinamento-perceptivo-motor.pdf Accessed 23 March 2017.

76 .THOMAS M. et al. Neural basis of alertness and cognitive performance impairments during sleepiness. Effects of 24 of sleep deprivation on waking human regional brain activity. **Journal of Sleep Research,** v. 9, n. 4, dec., p. 335-352. 2000.

77 .VAARA. J. et. al. The effect of 60-h sleep deprivation on cardiovascular regulation and body temperature. **Eur. J. Appl. Physiol**. n. 105, pp. 439-444, 8009. Doi 10.1007/S00421-008-0921-5.

78 .VINCENT, G. et al. Sleep restriction during simulated wildfire suppression: effect on physical task performance. **PloS one,** v. 10, n. 1, p. e0115329, 2015.

79 . WILSON D., BRACCI R. **The police agility test.** Law and Order 1982; 30:36 42

yes
I want morebooks!

Buy your books fast and straightforward online - at one of world's fastest growing online book stores! Environmentally sound due to Print-on-Demand technologies.

Buy your books online at
www.morebooks.shop

Kaufen Sie Ihre Bücher schnell und unkompliziert online – auf einer der am schnellsten wachsenden Buchhandelsplattformen weltweit! Dank Print-On-Demand umwelt- und ressourcenschonend produziert.

Bücher schneller online kaufen
www.morebooks.shop

Printed by Books on Demand GmbH, Norderstedt / Germany